MARKS &
SPENCER

barbecues
& salads

simple and delicious easy-to-make recipes

Lorraine Turner

Marks and Spencer p.l.c.
Baker Street, London, W1U 8EP

www.marksandspencer.com

Copyright © Exclusive Editions 2002

ISBN: 1–84273–730–9

Printed in China

Produced by the Bridgewater Book Company Ltd.

Photographer Calvey Taylor-Haw

Home Economist Sara Hesketh

The crockery featured on the following pages can be
purchased at Marks and Spencer's stores:

page 45 – silver-rimmed plate, 02148/5386

page 65 – white bowl, 02733/4285

NOTES FOR THE READER

- This book uses both metric and imperial measurements. Follow the same units of measurement throughout; do not mix metric and imperial.

- All spoon measurements are level: teaspoons are assumed to be 5 ml, and tablespoons are assumed to be 15 ml.

- Unless otherwise stated, milk is assumed to be full fat, eggs and individual vegetables such as potatoes are medium, and pepper is freshly ground black pepper.

- Recipes using raw or very lightly cooked eggs should be avoided by infants, the elderly, pregnant women, convalescents, and anyone suffering from an illness.

- The times given are an approximate guide only. Preparation times differ according to the techniques used by different people and the cooking times may also vary from those given. Optional ingredients, variations or serving suggestions have not been included in the calculations.

contents

introduction

There is something wonderfully evocative about the smell of barbecued food: it can conjure up memories of lazy summer evenings on the beach, or delicious aromas wafting from a campfire in the countryside. Barbecuing has never been easier either: there is an ever-widening range of barbecue equipment available nowadays, and with the advent of portable and disposable barbecues, this method of cooking food has become extremely easy, cheap and quick.

Some barbecues use coals or hardwood, and others are electric. Always abide by the safety instructions that come with your barbecue, and be careful around naked flames and fuel. Keep children and pets away from the barbecue area, and position your barbecue so that the smoke will not be a nuisance to other people.

This book contains a delicious array of dishes, from sizzling poultry and meat and mouthwatering fish to an extravaganza of vegetarian meals and salads. To round everything off, there is also a stunning selection of quick and easy desserts. So whatever the occasion, whether you are travelling far from home or entertaining friends in your garden, there is something here to satisfy every appetite.

guide to recipe key		
	very easy	Recipes are graded as follows: 1 pea = easy; 2 peas = very easy; 3 peas = extremely easy.
	serves 4	Recipes generally serve four people. Simply halve the ingredients to serve two, taking care not to mix imperial and metric measurements.
	10 minutes	Preparation time. Where marinating, chilling or cooling are involved, these times have been added on separately: eg, 15 minutes + 30 minutes to marinate.
	10 minutes	Cooking time. Cooking times don't include the cooking of side dishes or accompaniments served with the main dishes.

chicken satay skewers with lime
page 16

oriental prawn skewers
page 42

tabbouleh
page 74

stuffed figs
page 92

poultry
& meat

Barbecuing is a delicious way of cooking a variety of different meats and poultry, and an easy and satisfying way to prepare meals. The poultry and meat dishes in this chapter are all simple to prepare and quick to cook, and the sheer variety of accompanying ingredients and marinades ensures that there will always be an exciting assortment of flavoursome, mouthwatering dishes for your barbecue.

spicy barbecued chicken

		ingredients	
very easy	MARINADE	4 garlic cloves, chopped
	1½ tbsp chilli oil	1 green chilli and 1 red chilli, deseeded
	½ tsp brown sugar	
serves 4	½ tsp salt	CHICKEN
	1½ tsp mixed spice	4 skinless, boneless chicken breasts,
	1½ tsp dried mixed herbs	cut into slices
15 minutes	pepper	juice of 3 limes
+ 2½ hours	1½ tsp grated fresh root ginger	200 ml/7 fl oz water
to marinate	4 shallots, chopped	
	6 spring onions, trimmed and	wedges of fresh lime, to garnish
20–30	finely chopped	
minutes		curly green lettuce leaves, to serve

Put the chilli oil, sugar, salt, mixed spice and mixed herbs into a food processor and season with plenty of black pepper. Blend well.

Add the grated ginger, shallots, spring onions and garlic. Finely chop the chillies, add to the food processor and blend until fairly smooth. Transfer to a glass bowl, cover with clingfilm, and set aside.

Put the chicken slices into a non-metallic (glass or ceramic) bowl, which will not react with acid. Pour over the lime juice and water, then add enough marinade to cover the chicken. Cover with clingfilm and refrigerate for at least 2½ hours. Cover the remaining marinade with clingfilm and refrigerate until the chicken is ready.

When the chicken slices are thoroughly marinated, lift them out and barbecue them over hot coals for 20–30 minutes, or until cooked right through, turning them frequently and basting with the remaining marinade. Serve on a bed of green lettuce leaves and garnish with fresh lime wedges.

sweet & sour chicken wings

very easy	
serves 4	
5 minutes + 2½ hours to marinate	
20 minutes	

ingredients

MARINADE
2 tbsp sweet sherry
3 tbsp sherry vinegar or red
    wine vinegar
4 tbsp soy sauce
200 ml/7 fl oz orange juice
100 ml/3½ fl oz chicken stock or
    vegetable stock
50 g/1¾ oz brown sugar
pepper

1 tbsp tomato purée
2 garlic cloves, finely chopped
1 red chilli, deseeded and chopped

CHICKEN
1.8 kg/4 lb chicken wings

GARNISH
wedges of orange
1 long, red chilli, made into a flower
    (see below)

Put the sherry, vinegar, soy sauce, orange juice, stock and sugar into a food processor and season well. Blend until combined. Add the tomato purée, garlic and chilli and blend until smooth. Separate the chicken wings at the joints and put them into a non-metallic (glass or ceramic) bowl, which will not react with acid. Pour over enough marinade to cover the chicken, cover with clingfilm and refrigerate for at least 2½ hours. Cover the remaining marinade with clingfilm and refrigerate until the chicken is ready.

When the chicken wings are thoroughly marinated, lift them out and barbecue them over hot coals for about 20 minutes, turning them frequently and basting with the remaining marinade. Cut into a thick part of a wing to check that the chicken is cooked all the way through. If it is still pink in the middle, continue to cook until the chicken is thoroughly cooked. Garnish with orange wedges and a chilli flower (made by making 1-cm/½-inch slits in a chilli and soaking in iced water for 30 minutes until fanned out).

thai-style chicken chunks

		ingredients	
very easy		MARINADE	2 tbsp fish sauce
		1 red chilli and 1 green chilli, deseeded	1 tbsp lime juice
		and finely chopped	salt and pepper
serves 4		2 garlic cloves, chopped	
		50 g/1¾ oz chopped fresh coriander	CHICKEN
		1 tbsp finely chopped fresh	4 skinless, boneless chicken breasts,
10 minutes + 2½ hours to marinate		lemon grass	cut into small chunks
		½ tsp ground turmeric	chopped fresh coriander, to garnish
		½ tsp garam masala	
20 minutes		2 tsp brown sugar	freshly cooked jasmine rice, to serve

Put the red and green chillies, garlic, coriander and lemon grass into a food processor and process until roughly chopped. Add the turmeric, garam masala, sugar, fish sauce and lime juice, season with salt and pepper and blend until smooth.

Put the chicken chunks into a non-metallic (glass or ceramic) bowl, which will not react with acid. Pour over enough marinade to cover the chicken, then cover with clingfilm and refrigerate for at least 2½ hours. Cover the remaining marinade with clingfilm and refrigerate until the chicken is ready.

When the chicken chunks are thoroughly marinated, lift them out and barbecue them over hot coals for 20 minutes or until cooked right through, turning them frequently and basting with the remaining marinade. Arrange the chicken on serving plates with some freshly cooked jasmine rice. Garnish with chopped fresh coriander and serve.

sherried chicken
& mushroom kebabs

very easy		
serves 4		
15 minutes + 2½ hours to marinate		
15–20 minutes		

ingredients

MARINADE	KEBABS
50 ml/2 fl oz soy sauce	6 skinless, boneless chicken
2 tbsp sweet sherry	breasts, cubed
50 ml/2 fl oz vegetable oil	16 button mushrooms
1 tsp brown sugar	16 baby onions
1 tbsp honey	16 cherry tomatoes
1 clove garlic, finely chopped	
pepper	fresh flat-leaved parsley, to garnish
	freshly steamed or boiled rice, to serve

Put the soy sauce, sweet sherry, oil, sugar and honey into a large bowl. Add the garlic and mix until well combined. Season with plenty of pepper.

Thread the chicken cubes onto 8 skewers, alternating them with the mushrooms, onions and cherry tomatoes. When the skewers are full (leave a small space at either end), transfer them to the bowl and turn them in the sherry mixture until they are well coated. Cover with clingfilm and place in the refrigerator to marinate for at least 2½ hours.

When the kebabs are thoroughly marinated, lift them out and barbecue them over hot coals for 15–20 minutes or until cooked right through, turning them frequently and basting with the remaining marinade. Arrange the kebabs on a bed of freshly cooked rice, garnish with fresh flat-leaved parsley, and serve.

chicken satay skewers with lime

extremely easy	
serves 4	
10 minutes + 2½ hours to marinate	
15 minutes	

ingredients

MARINADE
100 ml/3½ fl oz soy sauce
100 ml/3½ fl oz lime juice
2 tbsp smooth peanut butter
2 tbsp garam masala
1 tbsp brown sugar
2 garlic cloves, finely chopped
1 small red chilli, deseeded and
  finely chopped
pepper

SKEWERS
6 skinless, boneless chicken
  breasts, cubed

GARNISH
fresh coriander leaves, shredded
wedges of lime

freshly steamed or boiled rice, or crisp
  green salad leaves, to serve

Put the soy sauce, lime juice, peanut butter, garam masala, sugar, garlic and chilli into a large bowl and mix until well combined. Season with plenty of pepper.

Thread the chicken cubes onto skewers (leave a small space at either end). Transfer them to the bowl and turn them in the peanut butter mixture until they are well coated. Cover with clingfilm and place in the refrigerator to marinate for at least 2½ hours.

When the skewers are thoroughly marinated, lift them out and barbecue them over hot coals for 15 minutes or until cooked right through, turning them frequently and basting with the remaining marinade. Arrange the skewers on a bed of freshly cooked rice or crisp green salad leaves, garnish with coriander leaves and lime wedges and serve.

tangy pork ribs

		ingredients	
easy	1¼ tsp salt	1 tbsp chopped flat-leaved parsley
	2 tsp paprika	1 tbsp sweet sherry
serves 4	2 tsp pepper	1½ tbsp brown sugar
	1.3 kg/3 lb pork ribs	4 tbsp Chinese chilli bean sauce
	1 tbsp chilli or vegetable oil	1 tbsp tomato purée
	1 onion, finely chopped	1 tbsp rice wine
15 minutes	6 spring onions, trimmed and chopped	1 tbsp sherry vinegar
	3 garlic cloves, chopped	100 ml/3½ fl oz orange juice
	2 tsp finely chopped fresh ginger root	2½ tbsp soy sauce
2½–2¾ hours	1 red chilli, chopped	salt and pepper
	1 tbsp chopped fresh coriander	wedges of orange, to serve

Preheat the oven to 240°C/475°F/Gas Mark 9. Combine the salt, paprika and pepper in a baking dish and then add the ribs. Turn them in the dish to coat them well all over. Cook in the centre of the preheated oven for 1¾–2 hours, then remove the dish from the oven, lift out the ribs, drain off the fat and set aside.

Heat the oil in a frying pan. Add the onion, spring onions, garlic, ginger and chilli and stir-fry over a high heat for 1 minute. Then add the herbs, sherry, sugar, chilli bean sauce, tomato purée, rice wine, vinegar, orange juice and soy sauce. Stir in a large pinch of salt and season well with pepper. Bring to the boil, lower the heat and simmer for 15–20 minutes, stirring occasionally.

To barbecue the ribs, coat them in the sauce, then grill them over hot coals for 7–10 minutes on each side, or until cooked right through, turning them frequently and basting with more sauce as necessary. Serve at once, accompanied by orange wedges.

curried lamb skewers

		ingredients	
very easy		MARINADE	1 red or green pepper, deseeded and
		2 tsp vegetable oil	cut into small chunks
serves 4		1 tsp curry powder	2 courgettes, cubed
		1 tsp garam masala	16 baby onions
		2 tsp granulated sugar	
		200 ml/7fl oz natural yogurt	fresh coriander leaves, to garnish
20 minutes + 8 hours to marinate			TO SERVE
		SKEWERS	freshly steamed or boiled rice
		400 g/14 oz boneless lamb, cubed	crisp green salad leaves
15 minutes		140 g/5 oz dried apricot halves	

Put the oil, spices, sugar and yogurt into a large bowl and mix until well combined.

Thread the lamb onto 8 skewers, alternating it with the apricot halves, red or green pepper, courgettes and baby onions. When the skewers are full (leave a small space at either end), transfer them to the bowl and turn them in the yogurt mixture until they are well coated. Cover with clingfilm and place in the refrigerator to marinate for at least 8 hours or overnight.

When the skewers are thoroughly marinated, lift them out and barbecue them over hot coals, turning them frequently, for 15 minutes or until the meat is cooked right through. Serve at once with freshly cooked rice or a crisp green salad, garnished with fresh coriander leaves.

thai-spiced beef
& pepper kebabs

		ingredients	
	very easy	MARINADE	3 spring onions, trimmed and
		2 tbsp sherry	finely chopped
	serves 4	2 tbsp rice wine	salt and pepper
		75 ml/2½ fl oz soy sauce	
		75 ml/2½ fl oz hoisin sauce	KEBABS
	20 minutes	3 cloves garlic, finely chopped	1 kg/2 lb 4 oz rump or sirloin steak,
	+ 2½ hours	1 red chilli, deseeded and	cubed
	to marinate	finely chopped	2 large red peppers, deseeded and cut
		1½ tbsp grated fresh root ginger	into small chunks
	10–15		
	minutes		green and red lettuce leaves, to serve

Put the sherry, rice wine, soy sauce, hoisin sauce, garlic, chilli, ginger and spring onions into a large bowl and mix until well combined. Season to taste.

Thread the meat onto 8 skewers, alternating it with chunks of red pepper. When the skewers are full (leave a small space at either end), transfer them to the bowl and turn them in the soy sauce mixture until they are well coated. Cover with clingfilm and place in the refrigerator to marinate for at least 2½ hours or overnight.

When the skewers are thoroughly marinated, lift them out and barbecue them over hot coals, turning them frequently, for 10–15 minutes or until the meat is cooked right through. Serve at once on a bed of green and red lettuce leaves.

greek-style beef kebabs

		ingredients	
very easy	1 small onion, finely chopped	fresh coriander leaves, to garnish	
	1 tbsp chopped fresh coriander		
	large pinch of paprika	TO SERVE	
serves 4	¼ tsp mixed spice	freshly cooked bulgur wheat or rice	
	¼ tsp ground coriander	mixed salad	
	¼ tsp brown sugar		
25 minutes	450 g/1 lb minced beef		
	salt and pepper		
	vegetable oil, for brushing		
15–20 minutes			

Put the onion, fresh coriander, spices, sugar and beef into a large bowl and mix until well combined. Season with salt and pepper.

On a clean work surface, use your hands to shape the mixture into sausages around skewers. Brush them lightly with vegetable oil.

Barbecue the kebabs over hot coals, turning them frequently, for 15–20 minutes or until cooked right through. Arrange the kebabs on a platter of freshly cooked bulgur wheat or rice and garnish with fresh coriander leaves. Serve with a mixed salad.

cherry tomato, ham
& pineapple skewers

		ingredients	
	extremely easy	1 tbsp vegetable oil	freshly cooked rice, fresh green lettuce
		1 tbsp white wine vinegar	leaves or crusty bread, to serve
	serves 4	1 tsp mustard powder	
		1 tbsp honey	
		450 g/1 lb cooked ham steak, cubed	
	10 minutes	450 g/1 lb canned pineapple chunks, drained	
		12 cherry tomatoes	
	10 minutes		

Put the oil, vinegar, mustard powder and honey into a bowl and mix until well combined.

Thread the ham onto skewers, alternating it with pineapple chunks and whole cherry tomatoes. When the skewers are full (leave a small space at either end), brush them with the honey mixture until they are well coated.

Barbecue the skewers over hot coals, turning them frequently, for about 10 minutes or until cooked right through. Serve them with freshly boiled rice, fresh green lettuce leaves or crusty bread.

barbecued pork sausages
with thyme

		ingredients	
	very easy	1 garlic clove, finely chopped	flour, for dusting
		1 onion, grated	vegetable oil, for brushing
	serves 4	1 small red chilli, deseeded and finely chopped	TO SERVE
		450 g/1 lb lean minced pork	fresh finger rolls
	15 minutes + 45 minutes to chill	50 g/1¾ oz almonds, toasted and ground	slices of onion, lightly cooked
		50 g/1¾ oz fresh breadcrumbs	tomato ketchup and/or mustard
		1 tbsp finely chopped fresh thyme	
	15 minutes	salt and pepper	

Put the garlic, onion, chilli, pork, almonds, breadcrumbs and fresh thyme into a large bowl. Season well with salt and pepper and mix until well combined.

Using your hands, form the mixture into sausage shapes. Roll each sausage in a little flour, then transfer to a bowl, cover with clingfilm and refrigerate for 45 minutes.

Brush a piece of aluminium foil with oil, then put the sausages on the foil and brush them with a little more vegetable oil. Transfer the sausages and foil to the barbecue. Barbecue over hot coals, turning the sausages frequently, for about 15 minutes or until cooked right through. Serve with finger rolls, cooked sliced onion and tomato ketchup and/or mustard.

spicy thai-style burgers

		ingredients	
very easy		20 g/¾ oz fresh breadcrumbs, white or wholemeal	1 small red chilli, deseeded and finely chopped
serves 4		1½ tbsp finely chopped spring onions 1 garlic clove, finely chopped 1½ tbsp chopped fresh lemon grass 1½ tbsp chopped fresh coriander	salt and pepper TO SERVE
15 minutes		15 g/½ oz almonds, chopped 15 g/½ oz peanuts, chopped	wedges of lemon and lime fresh shredded Chinese leaves hamburger buns
10–16 minutes		500 g/1 lb 2 oz minced beef	

Put the breadcrumbs, spring onions, garlic, lemon grass, coriander, nuts, beef and chilli into a large bowl and mix until well combined. Season with salt and pepper.

Using your hands, form the mixture into burger shapes. Barbecue the burgers over hot coals for 5–8 minutes on each side or until cooked right through. Serve in hamburger buns with wedges of lemon and lime and shredded Chinese leaves.

beefburgers with chilli & basil

		ingredients	
very easy		650 g/1 lb 7 oz minced beef	sprigs of fresh basil, to garnish
		1 red pepper, deseeded and finely	
serves 4		chopped	hamburger buns, to serve
		1 garlic clove, finely chopped	
		2 small red chillies, deseeded and	
10 minutes		finely chopped	
		1 tbsp chopped fresh basil	
		½ tsp powdered cumin	
10–16 minutes		salt and pepper	

Put the minced beef, red pepper, garlic, chillies, chopped basil and cumin into a bowl and mix until well combined. Season with salt and pepper.

Using your hands, form the mixture into burger shapes. Barbecue the burgers over hot coals for 5–8 minutes on each side or until cooked right through. Garnish with sprigs of basil and serve with hamburger buns.

fish & seafood

Fish is a very healthy food: it is rich in vitamins and minerals, and offers a nutritious alternative to poultry and meat. This chapter contains some delicious recipes that you can easily prepare and cook on your barbecue. It rings the changes with a variety of fresh fish including tuna, salmon and John Dory, and a wealth of accompanying ingredients and flavours from different parts of the world.

barbecued salmon

extremely easy	
serves 4	
5 minutes + 2 hours to marinate	
20 minutes	

ingredients

MARINADE
100 ml/3½ fl oz vegetable oil
100 ml/3½ fl oz dry white wine
1 tbsp black treacle
1 tbsp brown sugar
1 tbsp soy sauce
1 garlic clove, chopped
pinch of mixed spice
salt and pepper

SALMON
4 salmon steaks, about 200 g/7 oz each

wedges of lemon, to garnish

crisp green salad leaves, to serve

Put the oil, wine, black treacle, sugar, soy sauce, garlic and mixed spice into a large bowl and mix until well combined. Season with salt and pepper.

Rinse the salmon steaks under cold running water, then pat dry with kitchen paper. Add them to the wine mixture and turn them until they are well coated. Cover with clingfilm and place in the refrigerator to marinate for at least 2 hours or overnight.

When the steaks are thoroughly marinated, lift them out and barbecue them over hot coals for about 10 minutes on each side or until cooked right through, turning them frequently and basting with the remaining marinade. About halfway through the cooking time, add the lemon wedges and barbecue for 4–5 minutes, turning once. Arrange the steaks on a bed of fresh green salad leaves, garnish with the lemon wedges, and serve.

spicy john dory

		ingredients	
	very easy	AIOLI	2 garlic cloves, chopped
		4 large garlic cloves, finely chopped	2 shallots, grated
	serves 4	2 small egg yolks	1 small red chilli, deseeded and
		225 ml/8 fl oz extra-virgin olive oil	chopped
		2 tbsp lemon juice	1 tbsp lemon juice
	15 minutes	1 tbsp Dijon mustard	
		1 tbsp chopped fresh tarragon	wedges of lemon, to garnish
		salt and pepper	
			TO SERVE
	15 minutes	JOHN DORY	crisp green salad leaves
		2 John Dory, filleted	raw and lightly blanched vegetables

To make the aioli, put the garlic and egg yolks into a food processor and process until well blended. With the motor running, slowly pour in the olive oil through the feeder tube until a thick mayonnaise forms. Add the lemon juice, mustard, tarragon and seasoning, and blend until smooth. Transfer to a non-metallic (glass or ceramic) bowl, which will not react with acid, cover with clingfilm and refrigerate until ready to serve.

Rinse the fish under cold running water, then pat dry with kitchen paper. In a separate bowl, mix together the garlic, shallots, chilli and lemon juice. Rub the shallot mixture onto both sides of the fillets, then barbecue them over hot coals for about 15 minutes or until cooked right through, turning them once. Arrange the steaks on a bed of crisp green salad leaves, garnish with lemon wedges, and serve separately with the aioli and the vegetables for dipping.

tuna & tarragon skewers

	extremely easy	
	serves 4	
	10 minutes + 30 minutes to marinate	
	10 minutes	

ingredients

MARINADE
2 tbsp white wine
3 tbsp balsamic vinegar
1 tbsp extra-virgin olive oil
1 garlic clove, finely chopped
salt and pepper

SKEWERS
300 g/10½ oz fresh tuna steaks
450 g/1 lb button mushrooms

chopped fresh tarragon, to garnish

TO SERVE
freshly cooked rice
mixed salad

Put the wine, vinegar, olive oil and garlic into a large bowl and mix until well combined. Season with salt and pepper to taste.

Rinse the tuna steaks under cold running water and pat dry with kitchen paper. Cut them into small cubes. Wipe the mushrooms clean with kitchen paper. Thread the tuna cubes onto skewers, alternating them with the button mushrooms. When the skewers are full (leave a small space at either end), transfer them to the bowl and turn them in the wine mixture until they are well coated. Cover with clingfilm and place in the refrigerator to marinate for at least 30 minutes.

Barbecue the skewers over hot coals for about 10 minutes or until the tuna is cooked right through (but do not overcook), turning them frequently and basting with the remaining marinade. Arrange the skewers on a bed of rice, garnish with chopped fresh tarragon and serve with a mixed salad.

oriental prawn skewers

very easy	
serves 4	
15 minutes + 2 hours to marinate	
4–5 minutes	

ingredients

MARINADE
100 ml/3½ fl oz vegetable oil
2 tbsp chilli oil
50 ml/2 fl oz lemon juice
1 tbsp rice wine or sherry
2 spring onions, trimmed and finely chopped
2 garlic cloves, finely chopped
1 tbsp grated fresh root ginger
1 tbsp chopped fresh lemon grass

2 tbsp chopped fresh coriander
salt and pepper

SKEWERS
1 kg/2 lb 4 oz large prawns, peeled and deveined, but with tails left on

GARNISH
wedges of lemon
chopped fresh chives

freshly cooked jasmine rice, to serve

Put the oils, lemon juice, rice wine, spring onions, garlic, ginger, lemon grass and coriander into a food processor and season well with salt and pepper. Process until smooth, then transfer to a non-metallic (glass or ceramic) bowl, which will not react with acid.

Add the prawns to the bowl and turn them in the mixture until they are well coated. Cover with clingfilm and place in the refrigerator to marinate for at least 2 hours.

When the prawns are thoroughly marinated, lift them out and thread them onto skewers leaving a small space at either end. Barbecue them with the lemon wedges over hot coals for 4–5 minutes or until cooked right through (but do not overcook), turning them frequently and basting with the remaining marinade. Arrange the skewers on a bed of freshly cooked jasmine rice, garnish with the lemon wedges and chopped fresh chives.

prawn & mixed pepper kebabs

		ingredients	
very easy		MARINADE	KEBABS
		2 spring onions, trimmed and chopped	24 large prawns, peeled and deveined,
serves 4		2 garlic cloves, finely chopped	but with tails left on
		1 green chilli and 1 small red chilli,	1 red pepper and 1 green pepper,
		deseeded and finely chopped	deseeded and cut into small chunks
15 minutes		1 tbsp grated fresh root ginger	
+ 3–4 hours		1 tbsp chopped fresh chives	wedges of lime, to garnish
to marinate		4 tbsp lime juice	
		1 tbsp finely grated lime zest	freshly cooked rice or Chinese leaves,
4–5 minutes		2 tbsp chilli oil	to serve
		salt and pepper	

Put the spring onions, garlic, chillies, ginger, chives, lime juice, lime zest and chilli oil into a food processor and season well with salt and pepper. Process until smooth, then transfer to a non-metallic (glass or ceramic) bowl, which will not react with acid.

Thread the prawns onto skewers, alternating them with the red and green pepper chunks. When the skewers are full (leave a small space at either end), transfer them to the bowl and turn them in the mixture until they are well coated. Cover with clingfilm and place in the refrigerator to marinate for 3–4 hours.

Barbecue the kebabs over hot coals for 4–5 minutes or until the prawns are cooked right through (but do not overcook), turning them frequently and basting with the remaining marinade. Arrange the skewers on a bed of rice or Chinese leaves, garnish with lime wedges and serve.

sweet & sour polynesian prawns

	ingredients	
extremely easy	SAUCE	KEBABS
	300 g/10½ oz canned pineapple chunks	6 rashers smoked streaky bacon
serves 4	50 ml/2 fl oz soy sauce	225 g/8 oz large prawns, peeled and deveined, tails removed
	2 tbsp sweet sherry	1 red pepper and 1 orange pepper, deseeded and cut into small chunks
5 minutes	3 tbsp red wine vinegar	
	50 g/1¾ oz brown sugar	freshly boiled rice, to serve
8–10 minutes		

To make the sauce, drain the pineapple chunks and reserve the juice. Set the pineapple chunks aside for the kebabs. In a separate large bowl, mix together the soy sauce, sherry, red wine vinegar and sugar, then stir in the reserved pineapple juice.

For the kebabs, cut the bacon rashers into small pieces and wrap a piece around each prawn. Thread the prawns onto skewers, alternating them with pieces of red and orange pepper and the reserved pineapple chunks. When the skewers are full (leave a small space at either end), transfer them to the large bowl and turn them in the mixture until they are well coated.

Barbecue the kebabs over hot coals for 8–10 minutes or until the prawns are cooked right through (but do not overcook), turning them frequently and brushing with more sauce as necessary. Arrange the kebabs on a bed of freshly cooked rice and serve at once.

vegetarian
& salads

Vegetarian cooking has really come into its own in recent years, and what better way to celebrate its versatility and diversity than on the barbecue? There has never been a better time for experimenting with new ingredients and combinations, especially with the ever-widening range of delicious vegetables and fruits now available to us. This chapter provides some mouthwatering vegetarian dishes to tempt your palate, and an exciting selection of salads which make wonderful barbecue accompaniments or light meals in themselves.

vegetarian mushroom
& pear skewers

very easy	
serves 4	
10 minutes + 1 hour to marinate	
5 minutes	

ingredients

MARINADE
2 tbsp extra-virgin olive oil
1 tbsp balsamic vinegar
1 garlic clove, finely chopped
salt and pepper

SKEWERS
750 g/1 lb 10 oz mycroprotein (Quorn™)
  pieces, or mycroprotein fillets
  cut into small chunks

450 g/1 lb button mushrooms
1 large pear, cored and cut into
  small chunks

wedges of pear, to garnish

TO SERVE
fresh green and red lettuce leaves
fresh crusty bread

Put the oil, vinegar and garlic into a large bowl. Season with salt and pepper and mix until well combined.

Thread the mycroprotein (Quorn™) pieces onto skewers, alternating them with the mushrooms and pear chunks. When the skewers are full (leave a small space at either end), transfer them to the bowl and turn them in the mixture until they are well coated. Cover with clingfilm and place in the refrigerator to marinate for at least 1 hour.

Barbecue the skewers over hot coals for about 5 minutes or until the mycroprotein (Quorn™) is cooked right through, turning them frequently and basting with the remaining marinade. Arrange the skewers on a bed of fresh green and red lettuce leaves, garnish with wedges of pear and serve with fresh crusty bread.

bean & vegetable burgers
with tomato salsa

		ingredients	
	very easy	**BURGERS**	**SALSA**
		200 g/7 oz canned chickpeas, drained and rinsed	4 large tomatoes, chopped
	serves 4	200 g/7 oz canned cannellini beans, drained and rinsed	1 tbsp lime juice
			2 shallots, peeled and chopped
			1 garlic clove, peeled and chopped
	15 minutes + 30 minutes to chill	1 large courgette, finely grated	1 tbsp chopped fresh basil
		1 large carrot, peeled and finely grated	
		1 garlic clove, peeled and finely chopped	**GARNISH**
			chopped fresh basil
	10–20 minutes	85 g/3 oz breadcrumbs	wedges of lime
		salt and pepper	hamburger buns, to serve

Put the chickpeas and cannellini beans into a food processor and blend together briefly. Transfer to a large bowl, then add the courgette, carrot, garlic and breadcrumbs. Season with salt and pepper, then mix together until thoroughly combined. Using your hands, form the mixture into burger shapes, transfer to a shallow dish and cover with clingfilm. Refrigerate for 30 minutes.

To make the salsa, put the tomatoes, lime juice, shallots, garlic and basil into a bowl and stir together. Cover with clingfilm and set aside.

Barbecue the burgers over hot coals for 5–10 minutes on each side or until cooked right through. Remove from the coals and transfer to serving plates. Garnish with chopped basil and wedges of lime and serve with hamburger buns and the salsa.

mixed nut burgers with chilli

		ingredients	
easy	200 ml/7 fl oz boiling water	1 tsp dried mixed herbs	
	2 tbsp soy sauce	1 tbsp tomato purée	
serves 4	200 g/7 oz bulgur wheat	4 eggs	
	100 g/3½ oz cashew nuts		
	100 g/3½ oz hazelnuts	TO SERVE	
25 minutes	50 g/1¾ oz almonds	hamburger buns	
+ 3 hours	1 garlic clove, grated	slices of tomato	
to chill	1 small red chilli, deseeded and	chopped mixed nuts, toasted	
	finely chopped		
10–12 minutes			

Pour the boiling water and soy sauce into a heatproof bowl. Rinse and drain the bulgur wheat three times, then add it to the bowl and stir into the liquid. Leave for 15–20 minutes, or until all the liquid has been absorbed.

While the bulgur wheat is soaking, grind the cashew nuts, hazelnuts and almonds in a food processor. When the bulgur wheat is ready (and all the liquid has been absorbed), add the ground nuts to the bowl and stir them in. Then add the garlic, chilli, mixed herbs, tomato purée and eggs and mix until well combined. Cover with clingfilm and refrigerate for 3 hours.

When the mixture has chilled, form it into burger shapes, then barbecue over hot coals for 10–12 minutes or until cooked through, turning once. About halfway through the cooking time, add the tomato slices. Barbecue for 4–5 minutes, turning once. Serve at once with hamburger buns, the tomato slices and chopped nuts.

stuffed tortillas

easy	
serves 4	
10–15 minutes	
15–17 minutes	

ingredients

2 red peppers, deseeded and cut
    into quarters
4 vegetarian sausages
325 g/11½ oz canned red kidney
    beans, drained, rinsed, and
    drained again
4 large tomatoes, chopped
1 large onion, chopped
1 garlic clove, chopped
1 tbsp lime juice

1 tbsp chopped fresh basil
salt and pepper
4 large wheat or corn tortillas,
    or 8 small ones

TO SERVE
shredded lettuce
slices of fresh tomato
soured cream

Cook the red peppers on the barbecue, skin side down, for about 5 minutes or until the skins are blackened and charred. Transfer them to a polythene bag, seal the bag and set to one side.

Barbecue the sausages over hot coals for 10–12 minutes or until cooked right through, turning occasionally. While the sausages are cooking, put the kidney beans, tomatoes, onion, garlic, lime juice and basil into a large bowl. Season with salt and pepper and mix until well combined.

Take the red pepper quarters from the polythene bag and remove the blackened skins. Chop the flesh into small pieces and add it to the kidney bean mixture. About one minute before the sausages are ready, warm the tortillas on the barbecue for a few seconds.

Remove the sausages from the barbecue and cut them into slices. Fill the tortillas with sausage slices, kidney bean salsa, shredded lettuce, tomato slices and soured cream. Serve at once.

haloumi cheese
& vegetable kebabs

		ingredients	
very easy			
		MARINADE	12 cherry tomatoes
		4 tbsp extra-virgin olive oil	2 courgettes, cut into small chunks
serves 4		2 tbsp balsamic vinegar	1 red pepper, deseeded and cut into
		2 garlic cloves, finely chopped	small chunks
		1 tbsp chopped fresh coriander	
		salt and pepper	chopped fresh coriander, to garnish
10 minutes +			
2–2½ hours		KEBABS	TO SERVE
to marinate		225 g/8 oz haloumi cheese	freshly cooked rice or salad leaves
		12 button mushrooms	fresh crusty bread
5–10 minutes		8 baby onions	

Put the oil, vinegar, garlic and coriander into a large bowl. Season with salt and pepper and mix until well combined.

Cut the haloumi cheese into bite-sized cubes. Thread the cubes onto skewers, alternating them with whole button mushrooms, baby onions, cherry tomatoes, and courgette and red pepper chunks. When the skewers are full (leave a small space at either end), transfer them to the bowl and turn them in the mixture until they are well coated. Cover with clingfilm and place in the refrigerator to marinate for at least 2 hours.

When the skewers are thoroughly marinated, barbecue them over hot coals for 5–10 minutes or until they are cooked to your taste, turning them frequently and basting with the remaining marinade. Arrange the skewers on a bed of freshly cooked rice or fresh mixed salad leaves, garnish with coriander leaves and serve with fresh crusty bread.

chilli beanburgers
with onion salsa

easy		
serves 4		
15–20 minutes		
10–20 minutes		

ingredients

SALSA
4 large tomatoes, chopped
1 red onion, finely chopped
1 garlic clove, chopped
1 tbsp chopped fresh coriander
1 tbsp chopped fresh flat-leaved
  parsley
1 tbsp red wine vinegar
1 tbsp lime juice
salt and pepper

BURGERS
225 g/8 oz canned red kidney beans
1 large carrot, boiled and mashed
1 large red onion, finely chopped
25 g/1 oz fresh breadcrumbs
4 tbsp plain flour
1 tbsp tomato purée
sprigs of fresh coriander and wedges
  of lime, to garnish
hamburger buns and vegetarian cheese
  slices, to serve

To make the salsa, put the tomatoes, onion, garlic, herbs, vinegar and lime juice into a bowl. Season with salt and pepper and mix until well combined. Cover with clingfilm and set aside.

To make the burgers, drain the canned kidney beans, rinse them, and drain them again. Put them into a large mixing bowl with the carrot, onion, breadcrumbs, flour and tomato purée, and mix until well combined. Season well with salt and pepper. Using your hands, form the mixture into burger shapes. Barbecue the burgers over hot coals for 5–10 minutes on each side or until cooked right through. Garnish with sprigs of fresh coriander and wedges of lime and serve with hamburger buns and cheese slices.

cheese & vegetable baps

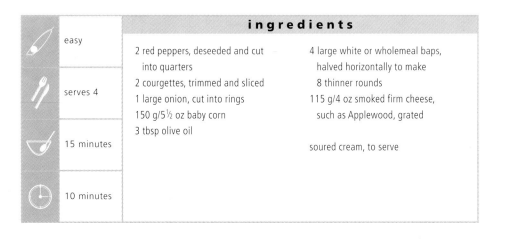

		ingredients
easy		
	2 red peppers, deseeded and cut into quarters	4 large white or wholemeal baps, halved horizontally to make
serves 4	2 courgettes, trimmed and sliced	8 thinner rounds
	1 large onion, cut into rings	115 g/4 oz smoked firm cheese,
	150 g/5½ oz baby corn	such as Applewood, grated
15 minutes	3 tbsp olive oil	
		soured cream, to serve
10 minutes		

Cook the peppers on the barbecue, skin side down, for 5 minutes or until the skins are charred. Transfer them to a polythene bag, seal the bag, and set to one side. Brush the courgettes, onion rings and corn with oil and barbecue over hot coals for 5 minutes, turning them frequently and basting with more oil if necessary.

While the vegetables are on the barbecue, take the bottom halves of the baps, brush the cut sides with oil and sprinkle over some cheese. Cover with the top halves, then wrap each bap in foil and transfer them to the barbecue. Warm for 2–4 minutes, just until the cheese starts to melt (do not overcook).

While the baps are warming, take the pepper quarters from the bag and remove the skins. Chop the flesh into small pieces and transfer it to a plate with the other vegetables.

Transfer the baps to serving plates and remove the foil. Fill them with the cooked vegetables and soured cream and serve at once.

spicy vegetarian sausages

		ingredients	
easy		1 garlic clove, finely chopped	1 egg yolk
		1 onion, finely chopped	1 tbsp chopped fresh oregano
serves 4		1 red chilli, deseeded and finely chopped	salt and pepper
			flour, for dusting
		400 g/14 oz canned red kidney beans, rinsed, drained and mashed	vegetable oil, for brushing
15 minutes + 45 minutes to chill		100 g/3½ oz fresh breadcrumbs	TO SERVE
		50 g/1¾ oz almonds, toasted and ground	fresh finger rolls
			sliced onion, lightly cooked
15 minutes		50 g/1¾ oz cooked rice	sliced tomato, lightly cooked
		50 g/1¾ oz Cheddar cheese, grated	tomato ketchup and/or mustard

Put the garlic, onion, chilli, mashed kidney beans, breadcrumbs, almonds, rice and cheese into a large bowl. Stir in the egg yolk and oregano, then season with salt and plenty of pepper.

Using your hands, form the mixture into sausage shapes. Roll each sausage in a little flour, then transfer to a bowl, cover with clingfilm and refrigerate for 45 minutes.

Brush a piece of aluminium foil with oil, then put the sausages on the foil and brush them with a little more vegetable oil. Transfer the sausages and foil to the barbecue. Barbecue over hot coals, turning the sausages frequently, for about 15 minutes or until cooked right through. Serve with finger rolls, cooked sliced onion and tomato, and tomato ketchup and/or mustard.

carrot, cabbage
& mixed fruit salad

		ingredients	
extremely easy		200 g/7 oz raw carrots	50 g/1¾ oz sultanas
		200 g/7 oz raw white cabbage	50 g/1¾ oz raisins
serves 4		100 g/3½ oz sprouting beans	1 tbsp lemon juice
		50 g/1¾ oz alfalfa sprouts	
10 minutes			
—			

Trim and peel the carrots, then grate them into a large salad bowl. Trim the white cabbage, then shred it finely. Transfer it to a large colander and rinse under cold running water. Drain well, then add it to the carrots.

Put the sprouting beans and alfalfa into the colander and rinse well, then drain and add to the salad. Rinse and drain the sultanas and raisins and add them to the bowl. Pour in the lemon juice, toss the salad in it, and serve.

beetroot, apple & celery salad

		ingredients
extremely easy		2 apples
		2 large or 4 small cooked beetroots
serves 4		2 celery sticks
		100 ml/3½ fl oz natural yogurt
5–10 minutes		1 tbsp lemon juice
—		

Wash and core the apples, but leave the skin on. Grate them into a large salad bowl.

Grate the beetroot, then add it to the bowl with the apples. Wash and trim the celery sticks, cut them into small pieces, then add them to the salad.

Add the yogurt and lemon juice, mix until all the ingredients are thoroughly combined, then serve.

avocado, sweetcorn & walnut salad

extremely easy		**ingredients**
serves 4		350 g/12 oz canned sweetcorn
		75 g/3 oz walnuts, chopped
		2 large, ripe avocados
		6 tbsp lemon juice
		6 tbsp soured cream
10 minutes		25 g/1 oz walnuts, chopped, to garnish
—		

Drain the sweetcorn, then put it into a large salad bowl. Add the walnuts and mix until well combined.

Peel, stone and cut the avocados into small pieces, brush them with some of the lemon juice to prevent discoloration, then add them to the salad.

In a separate bowl, mix the remaining lemon juice with the soured cream until a smooth consistency is reached. Add more lemon juice or cream if necessary. Add the lemon cream to the salad, stir it in, sprinkle with chopped walnuts, and serve.

broad beans with
mozzarella & basil

		ingredients	
	extremely easy	450 g/1 lb broad beans (shelled weight)	GARNISH finely chopped fresh mint
	serves 4	4 tbsp extra-virgin olive oil 1 tbsp lime juice 1 tbsp finely chopped fresh basil 60 g/2¼ oz firm mozzarella	wedges of lime
	10 minutes		
	2 minutes		

Bring a saucepan of water to the boil, then add the broad beans and cook for 2 minutes. Drain well and leave to cool.

In a separate bowl, mix together the olive oil, lime juice and chopped basil.

When the beans are cool, transfer them to a large salad bowl. Pour over the oil dressing and mix until well combined. Cut the mozzarella into cubes and stir them gently into the salad. Garnish with chopped fresh mint and lime wedges and serve.

tabbouleh

		ingredients	
extremely easy		200 g/7 oz bulgur wheat	chopped fresh parsley, to garnish
		½ cucumber	
serves 4		4 ripe tomatoes	TO SERVE
		3 spring onions	4 pitta breads
		100 g/3½ oz fresh flat-leaved parsley	wedges of lemon
25 minutes		100 g/3½ oz fresh mint	
		juice of ½ lemon	
1 minute			

Rinse and drain the bulgur wheat three times, then transfer it to a large heatproof bowl.

Bring a kettle of water to the boil. Pour over enough boiling water to cover the bulgur wheat, with about 1 cm/½ inch more on top. Set aside for 15–20 minutes, until the water has been absorbed.

While the bulgur wheat is soaking, prepare the salad. Peel the cucumber, cut it into small cubes, and transfer it to a large salad bowl. Wash and chop the tomatoes and trim and chop the spring onions, then add them to the bowl. Wash and chop the herbs, and add them to the salad with the lemon juice.

When the bulgur wheat is ready, squeeze out any remaining moisture and add it to the salad. Toss all the ingredients together and garnish with chopped parsley. Warm the pitta breads on the barbecue for a few seconds, then pass them round with the tabbouleh. Serve with wedges of lemon.

spicy tomato salad

		ingredients	
extremely easy		4 large ripe tomatoes	GARNISH
		1 small red chilli	sprigs of fresh basil
serves 4		1 garlic clove	wedges of lemon
		25 g/1 oz fresh basil	
		4 tbsp extra-virgin olive oil	fresh crusty bread, to serve
5 minutes + 10 minutes to cool		1 tbsp lemon juice	
		2 tbsp balsamic vinegar	
		salt and pepper	
2–4 minutes			

Bring a kettle of water to the boil. Put the tomatoes into a heatproof bowl, then pour over enough boiling water to cover them. Let them soak for 2–4 minutes, then lift them out of the water and allow to cool slightly.

When the tomatoes are cool enough to handle, gently pierce the skins with the point of a knife. You should now find the skins easy to remove. Discard the skins, then chop the tomatoes and place them in a large salad bowl.

Deseed and finely chop the chilli, then chop the garlic. Wash and finely chop the basil, then add it to the tomatoes with the chilli and the garlic.

In a separate bowl, mix together the oil, lemon juice and balsamic vinegar, then season with salt and pepper. Pour the mixture over the salad and toss together well. Garnish with basil sprigs and lemon wedges, and serve with fresh crusty bread.

mixed cabbage coleslaw
with fruit

	ingredients	
extremely easy	100 g/4 oz white cabbage	100 ml/3½ fl oz mayonnaise
	100 g/4 oz red cabbage	2 tbsp lemon juice
serves 4	2 large carrots	salt and pepper
	1 onion	
	25 g/1 oz sultanas	
10 minutes	25 g/1 oz raisins	
—		

Wash and shred the white and red cabbage. Grate the carrots, and finely chop the onion. Put all the prepared vegetables into a large salad bowl, then wash the sultanas and raisins and add them to the bowl.

In a separate bowl, mix together the mayonnaise and lemon juice, season with salt and pepper and pour over the salad. Mix all the ingredients together until well combined. Serve at once, or cover with clingfilm and refrigerate until ready to use.

potato, rocket
& mozzarella salad

		ingredients	
	very easy	650 g/1 lb 7 oz small new potatoes	DRESSING
		125 g/4½ oz rocket leaves	3 tbsp extra-virgin olive oil
	serves 4	150 g/5½ oz firm mozzarella	1½ tbsp white wine vinegar
		1 large pear	1 tsp sugar
		1 tbsp lemon juice	pinch of mustard powder
	10 minutes	salt and pepper	
	15–20 minutes		

Bring a saucepan of salted water to the boil. Add the potatoes, lower the heat and cook for about 15 minutes, until tender. Remove from the heat, drain and set aside to cool.

When the potatoes are cool, halve them and place them in a large salad bowl. Wash and drain the rocket leaves, cut the mozzarella into cubes, and wash, trim and slice the pear. Add them to the bowl along with the lemon juice. Season with salt and pepper.

To make the dressing, mix together the oil, vinegar, sugar and mustard powder. Pour the dressing over the salad and toss all the ingredients together until they are well coated. Serve at once.

desserts

Barbecued desserts are a special treat and provide a satisfying finale to any al fresco meal. Fruits, in particular, are very healthy and nutritious foods, and are delicious cooked over coals. This chapter contains some truly irresistible concoctions: some are light and refreshing and may include unexpected combinations, such as apple and melon kebabs; others are rich and indulgent, such as barbecued bananas covered with melting chocolate and a splash of rum. All are very easy and quick to make.

apple & melon kebabs

	very easy		
	serves 4		
	5–10 minutes		
	10 minutes		

ingredients

6 tbsp butter
1–2 tbsp brown sugar
pinch of mixed spice
½ melon, such as galia or charentais
2 apples
1 tbsp lemon juice

natural yogurt, crème fraîche,
   mascarpone cheese or ice cream,
   to serve

In a small saucepan, melt the butter gently over a low heat. Stir in the brown sugar and mixed spice, then remove from the heat and pour into a large bowl.

Cut the melon flesh into small chunks. Wash and core the apples, and cut into small chunks. Brush the fruit with lemon juice.

Thread the melon chunks onto skewers, alternating with pieces of apple. When the skewers are full (leave a small space at either end), transfer them to the bowl and turn them in the butter mixture until they are well coated.

Barbecue the kebabs over hot coals, turning them frequently, for about 10 minutes or until they are cooked to your taste. Serve with natural yogurt, crème fraîche, mascarpone cheese or ice cream.

chocolate rum bananas

	very easy	
	serves 4	
	5 minutes	
	5–10 minutes	

ingredients

1 tbsp butter
225 g/8 oz plain or milk chocolate
4 large bananas
2 tbsp rum

grated nutmeg, to decorate

crème fraîche, mascarpone cheese or ice cream, to serve

Take four 25-cm/10-inch squares of aluminium foil and brush them with butter.

Cut the chocolate into very small pieces. Make a careful slit lengthways in the peel of each banana, and open just wide enough to insert the chocolate. Place the chocolate pieces inside the bananas, along their lengths, then close them up.

Wrap each stuffed banana in a square of foil, then barbecue them over hot coals for about 5–10 minutes, until the chocolate has melted inside the bananas. Remove from the barbecue, place the bananas on individual serving plates, and pour some rum into each banana. Serve at once with crème fraîche, mascarpone cheese or ice cream, topped with nutmeg.

brandied pineapple rings

		ingredients
very easy		1 pineapple, peeled, cored, and cut into rings fresh mint sprigs, to decorate
serves 4		MARINADE 2 tbsp honey
5 minutes + 1–1½ hours to marinate		3 tbsp brandy 2 tsp lemon juice
10 minutes		

For the marinade, put the honey, brandy and lemon juice into a large, non-metallic (glass or ceramic) bowl, which will not react with acid. Stir together until well combined. Put the pineapple rings into the bowl and turn them in the mixture until thoroughly coated. Cover with clingfilm, transfer to the refrigerator and leave to marinate for 1–1½ hours.

When the pineapple rings are thoroughly marinated, lift them out and barbecue them over hot coals for about 10 minutes, turning them frequently and basting with more marinade if necessary.

Remove the pineapple rings from the barbecue, arrange them on individual serving plates and decorate with fresh mint sprigs.

summer fruit nectarines

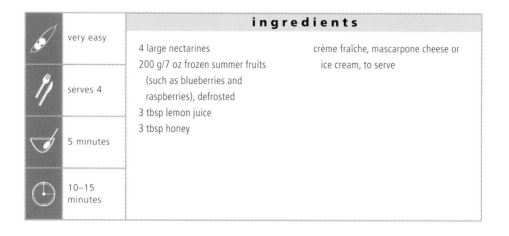

<table>
<tr><td>very easy</td><td colspan="2">ingredients</td></tr>
</table>

very easy	**ingredients**
serves 4	4 large nectarines 200 g/7 oz frozen summer fruits (such as blueberries and raspberries), defrosted 3 tbsp lemon juice 3 tbsp honey
5 minutes	
10–15 minutes	

crème fraîche, mascarpone cheese or
ice cream, to serve

Cut out eight 18-cm/7-inch squares of aluminium foil. Wash the nectarines, cut them in half and remove the stones. Place each nectarine half on a square of foil.

Fill each nectarine half with summer fruits, then top each one with 1 teaspoon of lemon juice, then 1 teaspoon of honey.

Close the foil around each nectarine half to make a parcel, then barbecue them over hot coals for about 10–15 minutes, according to your taste. Remove from the barbecue, place the nectarines on serving plates and serve at once with crème fraîche, mascarpone cheese or ice cream.

stuffed figs

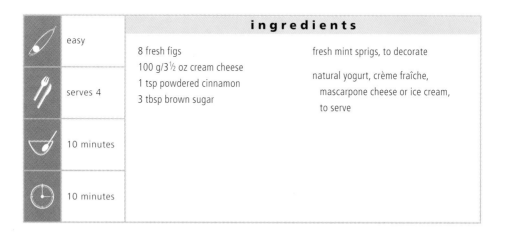

easy	
serves 4	
10 minutes	
10 minutes	

ingredients

8 fresh figs
100 g/3½ oz cream cheese
1 tsp powdered cinnamon
3 tbsp brown sugar

fresh mint sprigs, to decorate

natural yogurt, crème fraîche,
    mascarpone cheese or ice cream,
    to serve

Cut out eight 18-cm/7-inch squares of aluminium foil. Make a small slit in each fig, then place each fig on a square of foil.

Put the cream cheese in a bowl. Add the cinnamon and stir until well combined. Stuff the inside of each fig with the cinnamon cream cheese, then sprinkle a teaspoon of sugar over each one. Close the foil round each fig to make a parcel.

Place the parcels on the barbecue and cook over hot coals, turning them frequently, for about 10 minutes, or until the figs are cooked to your taste. Transfer the figs to serving plates and decorate with fresh mint sprigs. Serve at once with natural yogurt, crème fraîche, mascarpone cheese or ice cream.

barbecued apples

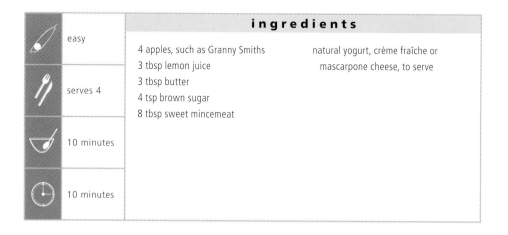

		ingredients	
easy	4 apples, such as Granny Smiths	natural yogurt, crème fraîche or
	3 tbsp lemon juice	mascarpone cheese, to serve
serves 4	3 tbsp butter	
	4 tsp brown sugar	
	8 tbsp sweet mincemeat	
10 minutes		
10 minutes		

Wash the apples, then cut them in half from top to bottom. Remove the cores and pips, then brush the cut sides of the apples with lemon juice to prevent discoloration.

Put the butter in a small saucepan and gently melt it over a low heat. Remove from the heat, then brush the cut sides of the apples with half of the butter. Reserve the rest of the melted butter.

Sprinkle the apples with sugar, then transfer them to the barbecue, cut sides down, and cook over hot coals for about 5 minutes. Brush the apples with the remaining butter, then turn them over. Add a tablespoon of mincemeat to the centre of each apple, then cook for another 5 minutes, or until they are cooked to your taste.

Remove from the heat and transfer to serving plates. Serve at once with natural yogurt, crème fraîche or mascarpone cheese.

index